Find the Truth!

Everything you are about to read is true **except** for one of the sentences on this page.

Which one is **TRUE**?

T or F   Three-quarters of South Koreans are connected to the Internet.

T or F   South Korea is the world's largest manufacturer of cars.

Find the answers in this book.

Contents

THE **BIG** TRUTH!

Robot Power

Masks often poke fun at specific members of society.

In 2006, six million tourists
visited South Korea.

6

South Korea

TARA WALTERS

Children's Press®
An Imprint of Scholastic Inc.
New York Toronto London Auckland Sydney
Mexico City New Delhi Hong Kong
Danbury, Connecticut

Content Consultant

Michael Robinson
Professor, Department of East Asian Languages and Cultures
Indiana University
Bloomington, Indiana

Library of Congress Cataloging-in-Publication Data

Walters, Tara, 1973-
  South Korea / by Tara Walters.
        p. cm. -- (A true book)
  Includes index.
      ISBN-13: 978-0-531-16855-4 (lib. bdg.)
               978-0-531-20729-1 (pbk.)
      ISBN-10: 0-531-16855-7 (lib. bdg.)
               0-531-20729-3 (pbk.)

  1. Korea (South)--Juvenile literature. I. Title. II. Series.

  DS907.4.W35 2008
  951.95--dc22   2007036023

Produced by Weldon Owen Education Inc.

1 2 3 4 5 6 7 8 9 10 R 17 16 15 14 13 12 11 10 09 08

CHAPTER 1

Country of Contrasts

South Korea is more popular among tourists than ever before. Why is it suddenly such a hot spot? Perhaps it is the mix of old and new. In South Korea, skyscrapers stand next to ancient temples. Pop culture thrives alongside traditions that are thousands of years old.

More visitors to South Korea come from Japan than from any other country in the world.

These young women are proud of their latest high-tech gadgets.

The Korean Wave is what the new popularity
of South Korean pop culture is called. Suddenly, all
across Asia, South Korean TV shows, movies, music,
and technology are the hottest thing. People style
themselves after their favorite stars. The Korean
Wave is what's happening!

Yet many visitors to South Korea still find it to be the "Land of the Morning Calm." The term comes from the original Chinese written name for Korea. It is made up of the symbols for "morning" and "calm." For many travelers, it remains an accurate description of this country. South Korea is rich in historic treasures and unspoiled countryside.

Performers of a traditional dance take part in a celebration.

Mount Sorak National Park has mountains, forests, waterfalls, and temples.

CHAPTER 2

From Rice Fields to Robots

The top of Mount Sorak is reached by a steep, 808-step staircase.

China

North Korea

⭐ Pyongyang

Sea of Japan

⭐ Seoul
South Korea

Yellow Sea

Japan

South Korea takes up the lower half of the Korean **Peninsula**. North Korea lies to the north. Japan lies across the Sea of Japan to the east. China lies across the Yellow Sea to the west. Much of South Korea's land is mountainous. Most people live on coastal **plains** and river valleys on the southern or western coasts.

The South Gate of the old city now stands in the middle of Seoul.

Farms, Fishing, and Cities

Farmers work the flat land along the south and west coasts. Rice is an important crop. It is grown along these plains. There are also fishing villages along the coastlines. However, since the 1960s, many South Koreans have moved from the countryside to the cities. Today, about half the population of South Korea lives in Seoul and Inchon. Seoul is the capital. Inchon is a major port. Seoul alone has 10.3 million people.

Cold Winters, Hot Summers

South Korea's climate is milder than North Korea's. There is snow in winter, especially in the mountains. But the surrounding seas help keep the temperatures moderate. Strong winds called **monsoons** hit South Korea year round. Summer temperatures average about 80°F (27°C). **Typhoons** often hit the southern coast. These huge storms occur in July and August.

People come from all over South Korea to enjoy the beaches of Pusan (poo-sahn).

Typhoon!

In summer, typhoons often strike South Korea. Typhoons are hurricanes in the western Pacific Ocean. In 2003, Typhoon Maemi struck South Korea's southern coast. It did a huge amount of damage to the city of Pusan. This is the country's largest port.

Almost 300 ships were damaged. A cruise ship was lifted onto a beach! Mud slides covered roads. A train was derailed. Twenty-eight passengers were killed. In all, at least 117 people died. About 25,000 people were forced to leave their homes.

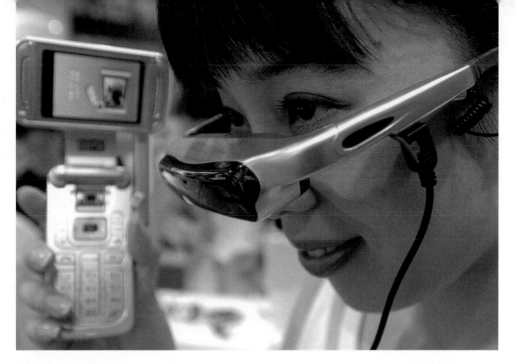

South Korea makes high-tech products. It produces cell phones and other communication devices.

An Asian Tiger

South Korea was once a poor country. Most people made a living from farming or fishing. However, starting in 1960, South Korea's economy boomed. It became one of the so-called Asian Tigers, along with Singapore, Taiwan, and Hong Kong. In Asia, the tiger is a symbol of power. These countries became very industrialized. They became major exporters.

Robot Caregivers

Different robots can do different tasks. Some robots help in hospitals. They deliver food and medical supplies to patients. Some robots help care for people at home. They can remind them to take medicine.

Robots and Robbers

Some robots guard homes. They have a digital camera in their head. If this kind of robot senses an intruder, it takes photographs. The robot also contacts its owner by cell phone.

THE BIG TRUTH!

Robot Power

South Korea wants to be the world's top robot nation. The country is working hard to earn this title. Its goal is to have a robot in every home by 2020!

Housework

Some robots can do household chores. They can vacuum the house. They can mow the lawn. They can also entertain the kids.

Human-Like Robot

Hubo is a robot made in South Korea. It is 4.5 feet (1.37 meters) tall. Hubo can walk, smile, and frown. It can also recognize voices and faces.

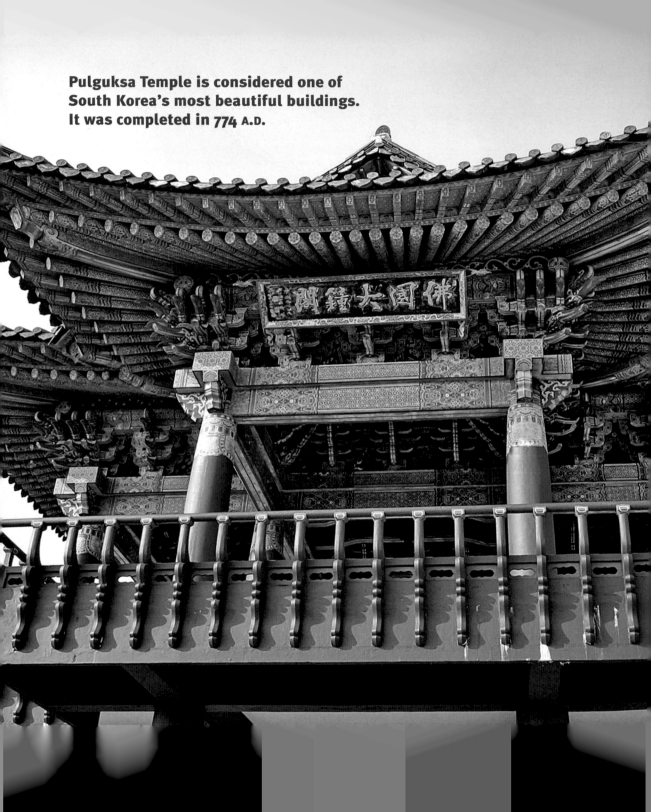

Pulguksa Temple is considered one of South Korea's most beautiful buildings. It was completed in 774 A.D.

CHAPTER 3

Thousands of Years, One People

In the late 1500s, the original wooden buildings at Pulguksa were burned to the ground.

People first settled on parts of the Korean Peninsula about 30,000 years ago. The **ancestors** of today's Koreans settled there about 5,000 years ago. Three states formed in the northeast, southwest, and southeast. They became known as the Three Kingdoms. During the Three Kingdoms period, Chinese culture spread throughout the peninsula.

Korean Kingdom

By 668 A.D., the Silla kingdom ruled the peninsula. Silla was a wealthy kingdom. It built great palaces and monuments. The royal tombs in Kyongju still inspire awe. The Silla made **Buddhism** the official religion. Buddhism is still widely practiced in South Korea.

This is one of the largest statues of Buddha in Korea. It stands at a temple in Seoul. The temple was built during the rule of the Silla.

In Buddhist art, the hand gestures are symbolic. The upraised right hand is the symbol for "no fear."

Kyongbok Palace was originally built under the Choson dynasty.

In 936 A.D., the Koryo **dynasty** replaced Silla. Korea takes its name from Koryo. During the Koryo period, Korean culture became increasingly distinct from that of the rest of East Asia.

The Choson dynasty was established in 1392. The arts, science, and technology flourished under the Choson rulers. Then, in 1592 and again in 1597, Japan invaded Korea. China helped Korea defeat the Japanese.

Modern History

By 1910, Japan had won control over Korea. The Japanese limited the freedoms and rights of the Koreans.

Japanese rule in Korea came to an end in 1945. This was after Japan's defeat in World War II. The victorious nations gave Korea its independence. They divided the peninsula into two parts. There was a plan to reunite the country. But it failed. In 1948, two governments were set up. North Korea became a **Communist** state. South Korea became a **republic**.

The Chinese symbol of universal balance is in the center of the South Korean flag. The groups of black lines around it represent heaven, earth, fire, and water.

Every year on March 1, South Koreans celebrate Independence Movement Day.

Torn Apart by War

In 1950, North Korean troops invaded the south. This was the start of the Korean War. Troops from the United States and other countries supported the South Koreans. The Soviet Union and other Communist nations supported the North Koreans. The war lasted for three years. After the war, the peninsula remained divided. No treaty was ever signed. The conflict between the two countries has not been resolved.

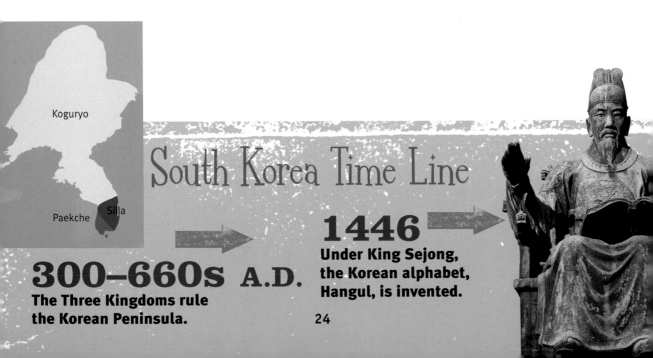

Koguryo

Paekche   Silla

South Korea Time Line

300–660s A.D.
The Three Kingdoms rule the Korean Peninsula.

1446
Under King Sejong, the Korean alphabet, Hangul, is invented.

South Korea Today

For more than 30 years, South Korea was ruled by military governments. However, in 1992, South Korea's citizens elected a new government. It fought **corruption**. It increased people's rights.

The relationship between North Korea and South Korea has remained tense. In 2000, the leaders of the two countries met. They pledged to solve their differences peacefully. Then, in May 2007, trains traveled between the two nations. It was the first time in 56 years. This event gave Koreans hope that some day their divided nation may be reunited.

1919

Yu Kwan-Sun fights for Korean independence from Japan. She dies in prison.

1988

The World Peace Gate is built for the Summer Olympics held in Seoul.

25

CHAPTER 4

Something Old, Something New

There is a rich tradition of ancient arts in South Korea. However, pop culture is putting South Korea on the map for young people everywhere. K-pop is South Korean popular music. It is a huge part of the Korean Wave. Stars, such as Rain and Se7en, are selling out concerts all over the world.

Se7en has even given a concert at Madison Square Garden in New York.

Music and Dance

Music in South Korea can be traced back to both traditional folk music (minsogak) and **court** music (jeongak). Minsogak is the music of the common people. It matches the rhythm of the heartbeat. Jeongak, on the other hand, was played at court. The rhythm of jeongak songs is slow and soothing. It imitates the rhythm of a person's breathing.

Jeongak songs are played on instruments made of bamboo and silk thread.

Nongak is the farmer's dance. It is one of the oldest dances.

Korean court dances follow strict styles. They have elaborate costumes. They were performed for the royal family. Today, they are still performed at official ceremonies. Folk dances vary from region to region. They use standard characters to poke fun at people, especially the upper classes.

Architecture

Since the end of the Korean War, South Korean cities have grown at a tremendous rate. Tall apartment and office buildings were built quickly. This was in order to house the thousands of people who were pouring into the cities. Some of these buildings are striking examples of modern design.

In traditional Korean architecture, design was always as important as function. Traditional architecture can be seen outside the modern cities.

These traditional wooden homes are in Kyongju. They were built to fit in with nature.

The ancient capital city of Kyongju is a wonderful example of traditional architecture. It is located on the southeast coast. The city is known as a "museum without walls." It has many ancient temples, tombs, and **pagodas**. The Pulguksa Temple is the most famous of these.

CHAPTER 5

Culture and Traditions

Some lantern floats are in the shapes of dragons or Buddhas.

Holidays and festivals play a great role in South Korean culture. Lunar New Year and the Harvest Moon Festival are both three-day holidays. Families gather in their hometowns. They honor their ancestors. Buddha's birthday is celebrated with the Lotus Lantern Festival.

Family is very important in South Korean
culture. Many families create memorial shrines
to honor ancestors. On important days, the family
will visit their ancestors' burial sites. Traditionally,
South Koreans were buried in coffins placed
upright in the ground. They were covered with
large mounds of earth. In ancient
times, Korean kings were buried
in this way.

**For the Harvest Moon Festival, more than
20 million people travel to their hometowns.
They go to visit the graves of their ancestors.**

People bring gifts,
such as fine foods,
to the graves.

This is a reenactment of Confucian state exams. For ceremonies like this, people wear the traditional costume of Confucian scholars.

The strongest influence in South Korean life is a philosophy called **Confucianism** (kon-FYOO-shun-izm). The principles of Confucianism govern much of people's conduct. Respect for elders is fundamental. So is the Golden Rule. This is to treat others as you would wish to be treated. Buddhism also has a strong influence. About 25 percent of South Koreans are Christians. This is the largest concentration of Christian believers in East Asia.

해설자 : 결혼식 날, 차르와 세 아들은 궁전 밖에 서 있었습니다. 세 왕자는 신부를 맞기 위해 오래 기다릴 필요가 없었어요.

소냐 : 소녀의 이름은 소냐입니다. 페테르 왕자님의 금화살이 소녀 아버지의 배 위에 떨어졌습니다. 그래서 소녀는 페테르 왕자님과 결혼하기 위해 이곳에 왔습니다.

올가 : 소녀의 이름은 올가입니다. 마르코 왕자님의 은화살이 소녀의 집 뜰에 떨어졌습니다. 그래서 소녀는 마르코 왕자님과 결혼하기 위해 이곳에 왔습니다.

개구리 공주 : 제 이름은 바실리사입니다. 개굴개굴! 이반 왕자님의 평범한 화살이 바바야가의 늪에 떨어졌습니다. 그래서 전 이반 왕자님과 결혼하기 위해 이곳에 왔습니다.

이반 : 아, 아냐, 당신은 아냐. 아바마마, 소자는 개구리와 결혼할 수 없습니다.

차르 : 결혼해야 한다, 이반. 약속이니까 말이야. (페테르와 마르코 왕자가 킬킬거리며 웃습니다.)

12

Language

Traditionally, Korean scholars used classical Chinese script for their writing. Chinese symbols express things and ideas rather than sounds. Then, in 1446, under King Sejong, a phonetic Korean alphabet was developed. This alphabet is called Hangul. It is still used today. Modern Hangul has 14 consonants and ten vowels.

Traditions

In ancient times, Koreans used a calendar based on the moon. Since tradition is important for South Koreans, many still use the lunar calendar for birthdays and holidays. Traditional clothing is often worn on holidays. It is also worn for important events, such as weddings and funerals.

Wedding garments are usually red. Red is a symbol of good fortune.

These students are celebrating graduation from college.

CHAPTER 6

Work and Play

To get into college, students work hard. They often go to classes until midnight!

South Koreans take education very seriously. The country has one of the highest literacy rates in Asia. Ninety-seven percent of South Koreans graduate from high school. That is more than in any other nation in the world. Students compete fiercely to get into college.

Kite flying competitions are popular in South Korea. Kite flying is believed to bring good luck.

In kite fighting, people try to snag or cut each other's strings!

Free Time

South Koreans enjoy many of the sports played in the United States, such as baseball and soccer. The martial art of Korea is tae kwon do (ty kwahn doh). It is also very popular. Ancient sports include kite flying and yutnori. These are traditionally played on New Year's Day. Yutnori is a game of tossing sticks. It is more than 2,000 years old.

Sport or Art?

The martial art tae kwon do started in Korea more than 1,000 years ago. It is famous for its kicks. In fact, *tae* means "kick," *kwon* means "punch," and *do* means "art." However, as with most martial arts, tae kwon do is not just about physical skills. Students also learn respect, discipline, and self-control. Since the year 2000, tae kwon do has been an official Olympic sport. It is one of the few martial arts in the Olympics.

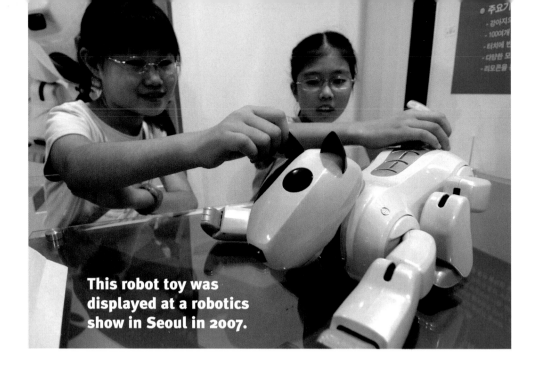

This robot toy was displayed at a robotics show in Seoul in 2007.

Well Connected

Today, almost three-quarters of South Korea's population have high-speed Internet connections. The government has spent billions ensuring access for everyone to the latest Internet technology. South Korea is known as the "most wired country on the planet." In many ways, South Korea is the face of the future. However, it will never lose the wonders of its long history and rich past. ★

True Statistics

Population: About 49 million
Population of Seoul: 10.3 million
International airports: Eight
Islands: More than 3,000
Internet users: 33.9 million
Currency: Won (wahn)
East Asia's third-strongest economy: South Korea
World's leading manufacturer of memory chips: South Korea
World's largest shipbuilding industry: South Korea
World's sixth-largest car manufacturer: Hyundai, South Korea

Did you find the truth?

(T) Three-quarters of South Koreans are connected to the Internet.

(F) Korea is the world's largest manufacturer of cars.

Resources

Books

Conway, John Richard. *Primary Source Accounts of the Korean War*. Berkeley Heights, NJ: Enslow Publishers, 2006.

Kummer, Patricia. *South Korea*. Danbury, CT: Children's Press, 2008. Enchantment of the World™, Second Series.

Lee, Cecilia Hae-Jin. *Eating Korean: From Barbecue to Kimchi, Recipes From My Home*. Indianapolis, IN: Wiley, 2005.

O'Brien, Anne Sibley. *The Legend of Hong Kil Dong: The Robin Hood of Korea*. Watertown, MA: Charlesbridge Publishing, 2006.

Sinnott, Susan. *Extraordinary Asian Americans and Pacific Islanders*. Danbury, CT: Children's Press, 2003.

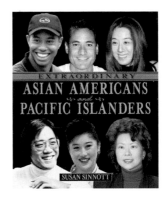

Stickler, John. *Land of Morning Calm: Korean Culture Then and Now*. Walnut Creek, CA: Shen's Books, 2003.

Taus-Bolstad, Stacy. *Koreans in America*. Minneapolis: Lerner Publishing Group, 2005.

Organizations and Web Sites

Asia Education Foundation: Korea for Kids
www.asiaeducation.edu.au/korea/kids.htm
Take a virtual journey around South Korea and try the quizzes.

TIME for Kids: South Korea
www.timeforkids.com/TFK/hh/goplaces/
main/0,20344,927166,00.html
Read all about South Korea and learn some Korean words.

Korean Food
http://iml.jou.ufl.edu/projects/STUDENTS/Hwang/home.htm
Find out the special ingredients in Korean food and try making
the recipes.

Places to Visit

Korean American Museum
3727 West Sixth Street
Suite 400
Los Angeles, CA 90020
213-388-4229
www.kamuseum.org
Learn about the history of
Koreans in the United States
and see work by Korean artists.

National Museum of Korea
135 Seobinggo ro
Yongsan gu
Seoul, Korea
82-2-2077-9000
www.museum.go.kr/eng
Visit South Korea's largest
archaeological and fine art
galleries.

Important Words

ancestor (AN-sess-tur) – a relative from the past

Buddhism (BOO-dizm) – a religion based on the teachings of Buddha

Communist (KOM-yuh-nist) – referring to an economic and political system in which the government owns all property

Confucianism (kuhn-FYOO-shuhn-izm) – a system of ethics based on the teachings of the Chinese philosopher Confucius

corruption (kuh-RUP-shuhn) – the act of being dishonest and unlawful

court (KORT) – a ruling family and its residence

dynasty (DYE-nuh-stee) – a series of rulers from the same family

monsoon – a seasonal wind that blows over the northern part of the Indian Ocean

pagoda – a temple tower with upward-curving roofs

peninsula – a narrow strip of land nearly surrounded by water

plain – a large, flat area of land

republic – a type of government in which laws are made by a group of people elected by the country's citizens

typhoon (tye-FOON) – a violent, tropical storm with high winds, occurring in the western Pacific Ocean

Index

About the Author

Tara Walters enjoys traveling to other countries and learning about their history, people, and culture. She loves history and geography so much that she studied it at the University of Notre Dame. She is a first-generation Irish American who spends part of each year in Ireland. Tara lives in New Jersey, with her sons, husband, and two dogs.